The Spirit of Creativity:

Inspirational Poems for the Creative at Heart

Ann Harrison

Copyright © 2019

Ann Writes Inspiration

All Rights Reserved

Formatting Copyright © 2019

Monarch Education Services

Cover Design Copyright © 2020

Tish Bouvier

Published by Ann Writes Inspiration

Dedication

For Jen,
Who challenged me to write poetry, even though I said
"I can't."

Acknowledgements

I'd like to thank the following people who helped me turn my dream of publishing a poetry book into reality:

First of all, Special thanks goes to our heavenly Father and our Lord and Savior Jesus Christ, for filling my soul and giving me divine inspiration to create these poems.

I'd like to thank Jen Lowry for formatting this book for print and running my manuscript through Grammarly and Pro Writing Aid, to help me catch any errors I might have missed during the revision process.

I'd also like to thank Tish Bouvier for helping me format the manuscript to publish as an eBook and for designing my cover.

Introduction
The Story Behind my Poems

"I can't write poetry! I have to dig deep within my soul for a poem. It's rare for me to write in this genre!" At least that's what I told myself until April 2019, when Jen Lowry, my sister in Christ and fellow writing warrior for Jesus gave her podcast listeners various poetry challenges throughout the month. In one particular episode, she challenged us to write a 50-word story. Her prompt was "mermaid fingernails."

After listening to this episode, I sat down and wrote my own story, which turned out to be 51 words instead of the proposed 50. But that didn't stop me! My brain separated the story into a poem, verse by unexpected verse.

From that point on, I was reading a lesson for Mark McGinnis's free 21st century foundation course which he talks about in his podcast called the 21st century creative. As I read the material, two other seaside poems formed in my mind. I was blessed to have written three poems in one day.

That week I had written five or six poems, some of which were inspired by Jen's challenges and others inspired and given to me by the Holy Spirit, either on walks or while sitting out on the front porch. There were a couple of poems inspired by Sue Vincent's "Thursday photo prompt", which you can read by visiting her blog at svincent.com.

After writing those first few poems, the more I told myself I couldn't write poetry, the more the Holy Spirit told me, "You say you can't write poetry, but you keep proving that you can."

Now that I've discovered my love for writing poetry, given to me by the Holy Spirit or inspired by a prompt/challenge, there's one thing I do when Satan whispers the following words in my ear: "You can't write poetry. Your verses aren't good enough!". I respond to this challenge with: "I can't, what? You see the poem(s) on my computer screen. Tell me that after I have written twenty some odd poems and published my first poetry book."

Now that I have put these verses in the following pages for your reading pleasure, I have a challenge for you. That's right, I'm passing the challenge given to me, down to you, dear readers. If you've always wanted to be a writer, but didn't know where to start, there's no time like the present. Use any or all of my poems as inspiration/writing prompts, then sit down and ask the Lord to fill your soul with the words that would be pleasing to Him. Once you've done this, close your eyes and listen for the words to flow like raindrops upon the blank page, forming inside your mind. As the words flow, let them flow from your heart, run down your arms, through your fingertips, onto the blank document with the cursor blinking at you from your computer screen.

If writing with pen and paper is for you, then take the same challenge above and let the words, given to you by the Holy Spirit, flow from your heart, down your arm to your fingers. Let your pen glide down each blank page as you fill it with the words the Lord has given you. Don't worry about spelling, grammar, punctuation or any of the proper writing rules and etiquette as you write, just get those words down. Remember, you can go back and edit later.

If you're not a writer, but you like doing other creative tasks, feel free to take the challenge into consideration and complete it in a way that fits your own creative style. Remember that we're not doing our work, simply to please the world or become rich and famous overnight. As Christian writers, creative artists and entrepreneurs, we've been called by God to use our gifts to share the message of His love and to tell others about the gift of Salvation.

In closing, I want to give you the challenge that I give my podcast listeners. I want to challenge you to read to get inspired, write something inspiring and share it with the world. For when you've touched one life, you've touched thousands. Don't let fear keep you from doing the work that God has chosen for you.

If you're sharing your work, inspired by this book, on your blog, website or social media, send me a link so I can share it with my tribe. Better yet, go ahead and pause right here, flip to the end of the book and follow me on social media. When you post what you've written, tag me in your post so I can share it on Facebook or retweet it on Twitter for all the world to see. Now that you've done that, come on back, curl up in your favorite pajamas and enjoy the following poems. I pray that each one blesses your heart in a special way as you read them. Happy reading, writing or delving into the creative gifts that God has blessed you with.

If you enjoy reading these poems as much as I've enjoyed writing them, I kindly ask that you leave a review on your favorite online retail site, on Goodreads or on your own blog or website. I'd especially appreciate it if you'd take a picture of yourself holding up the paperback version of your book and place it on your social media sites. Be sure to tag me and I'll share out your photos.

Hugs,

Ann

A Writer's Life

The following section is filled with verses about my journey from writer to author. I discuss everything from brainstorming to getting inspired by dreams, to self-doubt to realizing that I am now an author with several books published under my belt. As you read, consider your writing journey. Be sure to keep a journal handy, so you can write down any thoughts and ideas that come to you. Happy writing and may God richly bless you.

The Window to My Writing World

When you open my window
What will you see?
Pages and words
Dotted with bits of me.

Ideas that flow like raindrops
Upon a fresh blank page
Words that will forever
Last from age to age.

My characters take the stage
Bringing my story to life,
Filling page after page.

They fill my story
With plot twists and turns
leaving behind questions
Making readers yearn

To find the answers
In a book they can't put down,
Following each clue,
Until a solution is found.

Upon my mental movie screen,
It's hard to know which scene comes first,
My characters play them out so well,

I have to write them in short bursts.
As I mold, shape and revise each scene.

I can't stop writing,
Until I finish a book
For when you turn each beautiful page
You have a chance to take a look
Through the window of my writing world.

Brainstorming on the Front Porch

My phone dings to alert me,
Of Twitter tweets and chats.
Do birds tweet like we do,
Each trill a tit for tat?

Chimes ring out a melody,
Their song so soft and sweet
Singing with the birds,
Tweet, tweet, tweet.

Traffic hums on the highway,
Motors and big truck tires
Carpenter bees swarm around me,
Telling me of their desires.

The sound of children's laughter,
Their voices they do lift,
To make my front porch time
A special writer's gift.

Spontaneous Verses

The hum of the air conditioner,
The ping of my phone
There's a sound outside
That to me is unknown.

Oh, what could it be?
I can't look to see.
It sounds rather strange,
Yet harmonizing to me.

Is it a wind chime or bell?
Likely not, but do tell
The story behind it
If there's one to be found,
There's no hidden feeling
In the depths of this sound.

Does it matter to me,
What that sound might be?
Is it an odd bit of noise

Distracting to me?

I don't think so,
For its off in the distance.
A hum, soft and low
Heard from afar
By mere happenstance.

It may be a vehicle
Going down the highway,
I'm not quite sure,
But that's okay.

The sound inspired me
To write this simple verse
Without reason or rhyme
Never to rehearse.

Umbrellas and chairs
Out on the beach,
I'm stuck inside
Yet in my reach
My keyboard,
My iPad,
My iPhone screen
A song in my heart
My story in a dream.

My stories so short,
My novels so long,
It's high time to bring
An end to this song.

For I should be writing
And you should too,
Stories to tell,
And things to do.
This verse I shall end
With God bless you.

Creative Dreaming

Dreaming,
Creative dreaming,
Watching my story,
Unfold scene by scene.
Dreaming,
Creative dreaming,
My story unfolding
On a movie screen.

Is it possible
To see my story in dreams?
The people and places unfolding,
Like a movie scene?

Dreaming,
Planning and scheming,
My story develops,
Scene by scene.

Dreaming,
Planning and scheming
I write my story
Inspired by my dreams.

Inspired by Dreams

Dreams inspire me
To reach new heights
In my creativity.

I hear conversations
From people I don't know
I see their lives flow
Before me.

I'm taken to places
Against my will,
Yet further still,
I'm where I belong
At any given moment.

Though they don't make sense,
If I take my time
To watch the story unfold
Scene by scene,
Without reason or rhyme,
Images fill my mind
And characters tell me
What I need to know,
To make my story come alive
From a broader perspective.

The Flow of Words

*Words flow like raindrops
On a summer day,
Though sometimes they fly
Far far away,
Like unexpected scenes
Across the movie screen
Of my mind.*

*Drifting like a waterfall
My characters they tell me all
The things I need to know
For stories that I so
Long to tell.*

*It's my job to capture
The words I hold so dear
Before they disappear
To leave me far behind.*

*If I don't take my pen
And write these nuggets down
Slipping through my hands
They flutter to the ground
Like pennies being tossed
In a wishing well.*

While at other times,
They float upon the air
Inspire and make me dare
To write poetry.

How do they come to you,
In your creative zone
Racing like the wind
Or trickling one by one
As you sit all alone
In your writing space?

Rippling soft and sweet
Like leaves from a tree
They make my day complete
Heedless of the place
Where They find me.

Second Thoughts

I have second thoughts about my journey
The process of writing my story
Are the words that I placed on the page
Written for gods glory?

Give me oh, Lord, the words to write
Lay your story upon my heart,
These second thoughts don't seem right
Please give me a brand-new start.

What would you have me write today
To make my story ring true?
The words you Place upon my heart
I'll share to give all the glory to you.
Amen.

Sounds of Autumn

Wind chimes announce the changing season.
The drop in temperature gives me a reason
To write a glorious rhyme
As god's natural music
Keeps perfect time.
And to Him, may my words be pleasing.

Welcome to my Author World

I'm a writer,
I'm an author,
I'm a dreamer girl.
How do I tell people
About my author world?

Do I wear it on a t-shirt
Or on a special jewel?
Or speak it out loud,
No matter how cruel,
The world can be
To those of us who write?
Our minds keep creating,
Both day and night.

Writing our stories
And dreaming up new ones,
Over the years I've realized
I am not alone.

I've made writer friends
Who love to sit and talk,
About how their story ends.
And when they take a walk
Or drive in the countryside
Their stories are never finished.
Their thoughts wander far and wide,

Never to be diminished.

We're afraid to mention our author world
To those who don't understand,
But that doesn't mean we shouldn't
Try to take a stand
And tell the world of our calling
Given to us by God.
For we authors walk the path
Writers before us once trod.
Don't be afraid to tell the world
About your author journey,
For God has placed us in this world,
Made for writers Like you and me.

The Joy of NaNoWriMo

November has been set aside
For national novel writing.
Writers from around the world
Find this month exciting.

Novices and experts
Race against the clock
Words are counted every day
As time goes by, tick-tock

Will you get your 50k
Or will you fall behind
Writing your first draft
As November unwinds.

If you don't reach the monthly goal,
Don't worry, you're still a winner
To celebrate your daily word count
Why not go out with friends for dinner!

Come Join your Fellow WriMos

A story you must tell,
Write something new, revise something old
Break the rules and rebel!

The pressure's on, the stakes are high
To get those precious words penned down
You're not alone in your writing stride,
For writers hale from far and near,
You may find some in your own home town.

Will you come along with me,
My beloved writing friend
And join this challenge in November?
The furious writing doesn't end
Until the first day of December.

Seaside Poems

Come along and take a walk along the beach with me. Don't forget your journal, for each poem in this chapter has nuggets you won't want to forget. Let these poems be your guide as your muse takes you down a path full of uncharted creative territory.

Mermaid Fingernails

I stand on top of a sand dune,
Mermaid fingernails float to me on a wave.
A magical wind carries them away
Before I can gather my courage
To pick up the delicate shells
And place them in a bag I save
For trinkets I find on the shore.

The wind lifts them over the water
To find mermaids from whence they came.
I lost my only chance to capture
A shell that has never before,
Been gazed upon by the naked eye.

Will the mermaid fingernails appear once more
To be blown away with the tide?
In my heart forever more,
This precious memory I shall hide.

The Conch Shell

A large shell floats to me on the tide.
Before the wind can carry it away,
I pick it up and hold it to my ear
As the ocean waves subside.
I place it in my bag to keep
The sound of the ocean near
And forever in my heart I'll hide
This memory I hold dear.

Seashells

She sells seashells
By the seashore.
The seashells she sells
Are found on the ocean floor.

Seashells float to her on the tide,
Yet she explores the ocean to find
Seashells carried far and wide.

Leaving nothing to chance,
She'll explore
Sand and see,
Then at a glance
She spots a shell
Someone left behind

The seashell floats to her on a wave,
Crashing upon the shore.

She hides it in a special place
To keep it safe, forever more.

Ripples of Creativity

The sun shines on the water
Drifting out to see,
I sit in my deck chair,
My umbrella shading me.

The sand shifts beneath my feet,
Carried away by the tide,
As words flow like ripples
My fingers start to glide

Along my iPhone screen
Within the app called Notes
To capture each precious word
Before the ideas float

Drifting away in the see
Of long forgotten memories
Disappearing into the abyss
Like ripples of creativity

Poems from the Heart

All of the poems in this section were given to me by the Holy spirit, though the inspiration for many of them came from various aspects of the world around me. Open your heart as you read the following verses and fill the blank page of your journal, notebook, or the blank screen of a document or notes app on your computer or mobile device, with the words that flow from your heart. Stop and reflect on what these verses mean in your own life. May God richly bless you with wisdom and peace as you delve deep into the heart of the verses below.

New Beginnings

Some days you feel the end is near,
But let me tell you God is here
To give you a new beginning
When you feel as if the world is spinning
Out of control.

When our past seems to trap us,
We give it all to Jesus
He takes away the old
And renews your soul
To make you whole.
Remember Jesus loves you.

My Walk with the Lord

A gentle early morning breeze
Plants its kiss upon my face,
The morning sun shines down on me,
Its light will not erase
My most precious memory
Of God's amazing grace
As I call the name of Jesus.

As I take my morning walk
I lift my voice in prayer,
My Lord and I will have a talk
I'll tell him of my cares.

I'll start my conversation
With words of love and praise,
And in my meditation
I'll stop and feel the rays
Of the morning sun upon my face.

I'll pray for friends and loved ones
As God's amazing grace
Reaches down to touch them
In His own special way.

I'll stop to hear the melody
Of my front porch chimes
As they sing their song to me,

Without reason, without rhyme.

Thus, ends my morning walk outside,
But not my walk with God,
He'll always be there by my side,
Leading me to walk the path
Where heavenly angels trod.

Will you walk with God today
And let Him give you rest?
Will you take his yoke upon you,
Will you hear him and be blessed?

I pray the Holy Spirit
Will through my words impart,
His gentle loving kindness
To heal your troubled heart.

May God's love surround you,
May my words ring true,
Today I say a special prayer
God, bless, you!

Night Fall

Darkness falls as the sun sinks behind the clouds
Birds fall silent as they tuck their heads beneath their wings
The Earth is covered in shadow,
As the stars glide soundlessly across the sky
The moon follows in close proximity,
Covering the world in a nightly glow
It's time to drift into the world of dreams,
As you lay your head to rest
In preparation for the new day.
God's grace is sufficient for you
Until you reach your journey's end,
Blessed be the name of the Lord!
Amen.

Tears of an Angel

Her sorrows deep and silent,
Her tears fall at night,
Her smile shines by day.
Her mourning, low and tender,
Her weeping out of sight
As she pushes her pain away.

Can she hide her sorrow?
Can she dry her tears
And hide her pain from the naked eye?
The Lord sees and knows all,
Her pain, her fear, her sorrow,
He hears her anguished cry.

Come unto me, my child
For I will give you rest,
Give me all your sorrows,
Hear me and be blessed.

Give me your tears,
Your pain,
Your weeping in the night.
And I will give you joy
In the morning light.

Her tears are tears of joy,
Her pain has melted away.

The smile that shines for others
Is one of true happiness
On this bright blessed day.

Do you have pain
You mask with fake smiles?
Give it to Jesus,
He will heal you, my child.

And He will set you free
So your light shines through,
Your joy tried and true,
So you can share His love
With a lost and dying world.

Angel's Song

The voice of an angel
Cries so sweet and tender
The song of an angel
Rings through the night,
The words of an angel,
Fills my heart with sweet surrender,
And I long to take
My heavenly flight.

Lord, what would you have me do on this earth,
Before you call me home?
Your still, small voice fills my heart
With a melody like an angel's song.

Whisper words of Peace, so tender
That I might hear and obey,
The heavenly commandment You shall render
To my soul this very day.

The voice of an angel cries sweet and tender
To sooth my troubled soul this night,
All to thee, I surrender
Give me rest in your Holy light.
Amen.

Called from Darkness by a Rainbow

I stand in the shadow of the trees,
As through a colorful rainbow
The sunshine beckons to me.

Two trees make a triangle,
Through which I cannot see,
Unless I stare into the gap
At a lawn so brilliant and free.

Should I stand in the shadows alone?
Or find my way around
The trees pressed together
Into the morning sun?

Time seems to stand still
While pushing through the wall
I step out on the grass
The sunlight kissing my cheek
As beams of light fall
All around me.

I find I'm no longer alone
As bird song welcomes me.
Darkness turns to dawn
And in the light, I see
The rainbow fading away
Its colors dancing through the trees.

The day shines beautiful and bright
With a flag flying high in the breeze
As God reaches out His hand,
Through the darkness to rescue me.

Out in the open I now stand
My spirit flying free
To follow God's divine plan
And complete each creative task
Which has been chosen for me.

The Mysterious Path

What is this hidden path I see
Beneath an avenue of trees?
Where are the shadows leading me?

A mist obscures the path ahead,
I cannot see what lies beyond
Where my footsteps tread.

Should I turn away instead
Of following the sunlight's call,
Or should I take the road ahead,
Allowing the dim light to lead the way
And take the path unknown to all?

I travel down the darkened road,
Watching my footsteps as I go,
Through the thick, murky fog,
The shadows fade, as I trod,
Down this dark and lonely road.
Is this path an endless trail,
Or will I reach my destination?
I can't turn back, I cannot fail,
Yet I stand in hesitation,

Staring through the lonely shadows
That call to me once more.
Down this path I onward go,

Leaning upon the Lord

As I walk down this misty path,
A familiar face I see.
Who is this lonely traveler
Staring back at me?

Tears of joy course down my cheeks,
When those I love so dear,
As I grow ever closer,
Send up their joyful cheer!

The lonely path comes to an end,
The sunlight shines to greet me,
I see my family and friends
Who have come to meet me.
This is where my journey ends!

Snow Drifters

As I sit out on my front porch,
Surrounded by the autumn wind
I think about the coming snow
In faraway cities and towns
Where winter will soon begin.

I picture a small cottage
With a family seated by the kitchen fire.
As travelers drift along
To find their heart's desire.
I See these weary drifters
Walking through the snow
Following the distant light
Leading to the hillside cottage,
With a warm fire all aglow.

What brings these weary Travelers
Out in the winter wind
Are they on a mission
Where will the journey end?

Will they make it through the bitter cold
Or find shelter for the night?
Will they follow the beaten path
Or turn toward the fire light?

Let's pray they make it safely home

*In the blinding snow
Let the firelight Lead them
Where ever they must go.*

The Voice of a Singing Bowl

I play the bowl before I sleep;
It sings of promises I must keep.
It whispers its words of wisdom to me,
As it rings out a sweet melody.

One tiny note it does sound,
A melody in my heart I've found,
Easy to hum with no need for words,
As I play, the voice within my soul is heard.

It's there when I need it, day or night;
I play the bowl to my heart's delight.
This blessing from God fills me with peace,
My anxiety disappears in sweet release.

Not only at night do I play,
The bowl is a wonderful meditation
It gives me inspiration
For my writing day

When your life spins out of control
And the endless noise won't cease
Why not play a singing bowl
And pray for inner peace.

Spirit Song

The song fills my head as I play,
The bowl sings of things to come.
What does the song inside me say?

Is this song for everyone?
My close circle of friends?
Is it meant for me alone?
The questions never end.

The answers come slowly
A story unfolding.
The words take shape
As an image I'm holding;
On the screen of my memory,
Where dreams are clear to me.

What is this song
My heart must sing?
Does the melody ring
Within my soul?

Do I give voice
To the song expressed
Without a choice?
The Lord knows best.

No rhyme or reason,

No time or season
No words are needed
To say what I feel.
I know in my heart
The song is real.

Although some people don't believe
It fills the air,
Loud and strong.
Close your eyes and you'll receive
The healing vibrations
Of the spirit song.

The melody rings loud and clear
I sing it so that you may hear
The voice of a heavenly angel
Singing sweet words of piece,
Filling my soul with sweet release.

Hush!
Listen!
Rest in peace.

Author's Note

In this world, people are being discriminated against and excluded on the basis of their disability, race, gender, religious background and other cultural differences. I am blind; therefore, I know what it feels like to be discriminated against, and often times excluded, when it comes to finding employment and in other situations.

John 3:16 says: "For God so loved the world, that he gave his only begotten son, that whosoever believeth in him should not perish, but have everlasting life." In Matthew 19:19, Jesus tells us: "... *Thou shalt* love thy *neighbor* as thyself."

Small acts of kindness can make a significant difference in making others feel loved and accepted. Instead of turning away from someone when they are in need of assistance or staring at them because you don't understand their disability, open your hearts and show them love, by asking how you can help.

Learn more about how you can make the world a more inclusive place to live by visiting: https://lovehasnolabels.com

About the Author

Ann Harrison is the author of The Spirit of Creativity: Inspirational Poems for the Creative at Heart. Three of her previously published books are in the process of being revised and rebranded. She has also been published in several anthologies, including a devotional entitled God Things: Hope for the Hurting, alongside Jen Lowry and fifteen other authors. Aside from her work as a Christian fiction author, Ann is a professional freelance writer. She also hosts the Inspirational Journeys Podcast, where she gives authors, creative artists and entrepreneurs a platform to share their stories. When she's not interviewing special guests, she hosts solo episodes providing book reviews, reading selected poems, and sharing tips and encouragement for aspiring authors.

Connect with Ann

Visit her website at:
https://annwritesinspiration.com

Like her on Facebook:
https://www.facebook.com/annwritesinspiration

Follow her on Twitter:
https://twitter.com/annwrites75

Subscribe to her YouTube channel:
https://www.youtube.com/channel/UCbtievaVFrGUsuvlqlsPMOQ

And find her podcast on your favorite platform by visiting:
https://anchor.fm/inspirational-journeys

Made in the USA
Columbia, SC
24 August 2021